NATIONAL GEOGRAPHIC

School Publishing

Say Cheese!

PIONEER EDITION

By Susan Halko

CONTENTS

2 Say Cheese!

8 Changes for Breakfast

12 Concept Check

Say Cheese!

By Susan Halko

There are many kinds of cheese. In fact, there are hundreds. They come from all around the world.

All cheese begins with milk. How can you start with milk and end up with so many different kinds of cheese?

Science can help explain. Milk goes through big changes. They are **chemical changes**.

Two Ways to Change

Matter can come in three different states. They are solid, liquid, and gas.

An example is the way water changes. Water can be a liquid (drink). It can be a solid (ice). It can be a gas (vapor). It can change from solid to liquid to gas. It can change again and again. The way water changes is called a **physical change**.

Cheese is different. It's not just solid milk. It's brand-new matter. It cannot be changed back into milk.

Chemical changes happen when milk becomes cheese. Let's find out how this works.

From Liquid to Solid

First, milk needs to be a solid. Cheese makers add bacteria. Bacteria are tiny living things. You can only see them with a microscope.

Lactobacilli bacteria is added to milk.

The milk and bacteria are stirred. Then they are heated. Heat makes the bacteria more active. They turn the sugar in the milk into lactic acid. This makes the milk solid. It's like yogurt. That's a chemical change!

Next, cheese makers add rennet. Rennet is an **enzyme**. It's found in cows' stomachs. It makes the chemical change go faster. It makes the milk thicker. Now it's like pudding.

The milk is stirred while it is heated.

Curds and Whey

Solid milk is called curd. It sits in a liquid called whey. The whey is drained from the curds. Some curds are packed into molds. Salt is added. Other curds are heated. Then they are stirred again.

The whey is drained from the curds.

4

Cheddar the Cheese

Other cheeses, such as cheddar, are cut into slabs. They are stacked on top of each other. Then they are flipped. This helps drain more whey.

The slabs become thinner. They are cut into small pieces. They are salted. This process is called cheddaring.

Aging

Cheeses are stored in special rooms. The rooms have controlled temperatures and moisture. Aging can take weeks, months, or even years.

The bacteria are still alive in the cheese! The bacteria keep causing chemical changes as the cheese ages. They change the flavor and texture of the cheese. Cheese tastes sharper the longer it ages.

Cutting the curds into small pieces is a physical change.

The cheddaring process is used on different kinds of cheddar cheese.

5

Few Steps, Many Cheeses

The same basic steps are used to make all cheeses. But make a few changes, and you have a different cheese.

You can add some bacteria. There are thousands of different bacteria. Cheese makers decide which ones to use.

They also decide how much whey to drain. And they decide what temperatures to use. They decide to reheat the curds. Or not to reheat them.

Limburger cheese

The milk makes a big difference. Different breeds of cow make different types of milk. Or the cheese maker may choose goat milk. Or milk from sheep. Even buffalo milk can be used.

Let's see how to make a few famous cheeses.

Swiss cheese

Stinky Cheese

Have you ever smelled stinky cheese? It can knock your socks off!

That's because some bacteria in stinky cheeses are the same kind found in human sweat! P.U.!

But some stinky cheeses taste mild. Limburger is an example. It's stinky and tastes mild.

Holey Bacteria!

What makes the holes in Swiss cheese? Gassy bacteria.

The cheese is put in a warm room. The warm bacteria make gas bubbles. Another chemical change! The cheese holds in the gas bubbles. This makes the holes.

Blue cheese

Moldy Blue

What makes blue cheese blue? Mold!
It's added to the milk.

The mold reacts to oxygen.
Oxygen is in the air. The outside
of the cheese turns blue. That's a
chemical change!

But how do the blue lines get
inside? Cheese makers poke holes
in the cheese. Oxygen goes inside.
It makes the mold turn blue. That's
another chemical change!

As you can see, physical and
chemical changes are part of the
cheese-making process.

Wordwise

chemical change: a change in
matter that forms a new substance with
different properties

enzyme: a substance in plants or
animals that speeds up chemical
reactions

matter: anything that takes up space
and has mass

physical change: when matter
changes to look different but does not
become a new kind of matter

7

Changes for Breakfast

Chemical and physical changes happen all the time. They are even part of breakfast!

Let's look at a special breakfast menu. It will help you learn about the changes that happen in foods.

Review these hints about physical and chemical changes first.

Some signs that a chemical change has happened:

- Light or heat is given off
- The color changes
- Bubbling, or gas forms
- The odor or smell changes
- A solid forms
- The change cannot be reversed

Some signs that a physical change has happened:

- The substance is the same. Only its properties have changed

Good Morning!

Veggie Omelets

Melting butter in a skillet .... physical change

> *Butter changes from a solid to a liquid.
> But it is still the same substance.*

Shredding cheese .... physical change

> *Cheese changes its form. But it's still
> made of the same stuff.*

Chopping the veggies .... physical change

> *The physical properties of the vegetables
> changed. They were cut into smaller
> pieces. No new substance was made.*

Cooking the eggs .... chemical change

> *The eggs turn from liquid to solid.
> You can't reverse this change.*

Pancakes

Heating the batter .... chemical change

The batter changed. It was a liquid. It became a solid pancake. Pancakes cannot change back into batter.

Side Orders

Toast .... chemical change

Heat makes the bread turn brown and crispy.

Cold cereal .... physical change

Add milk to cereal. It's mushy. But it doesn't make it a new substance.

Physical and Chemical Changes

Find out what you learned about changes in matter.

1 What is a chemical change?

2 What is a physical change?

3 Why does Swiss cheese have holes?

4 Why do stinky cheeses smell so bad?

5 Is making waffles a physical change or a chemical change? Explain.